Plagues

by David Orme

Trailblazers

Plagues
by David Orme
Educational consultant: Helen Bird

Illustrated by Martin Bolchover

Published by Ransom Publishing Ltd.
51 Southgate Street, Winchester, Hants. SO23 9EH
www.ransom.co.uk

ISBN   978 184167 798 9
First published in 2009

Plagues

Contents

THE 'BLACK DEATH' ENTERED ENGLAND IN 1348 THROUGH THIS PORT.

IT KILLED 30-50% OF THE COUNTRY'S TOTAL POPULATION

Plagues

Get the facts

What is a plague?

A **plague** is **disease** that can spread from person to person.

What **causes diseases like this?**

These diseases are

bacteria

viruses

Bacteria

A **bacterium** is a tiny living thing. The world is full of them.

Luckily, most bacteria are harmless.

Some are good – many live in our bodies and help us digest food.

But diseases like **typhoid**, TB and **bubonic plague** are caused by bacteria.

Antibiotics are medicines that can kill bacteria.

Here are a few grams of soil. There are about **200 million bacteria** in it!

Viruses

Viruses are harder to ... they are much
... bacteria and are not killed by
... otics.

... es cause diseases such as
... and 'flu **smallpox** and **AIDS**

vaccine

... when it is
injected ... the body, it helps the
... learn how to deal with the
... illness when it comes along.

Some of these diseases are hard to
cure. No one has yet made a
... for the **common cold**

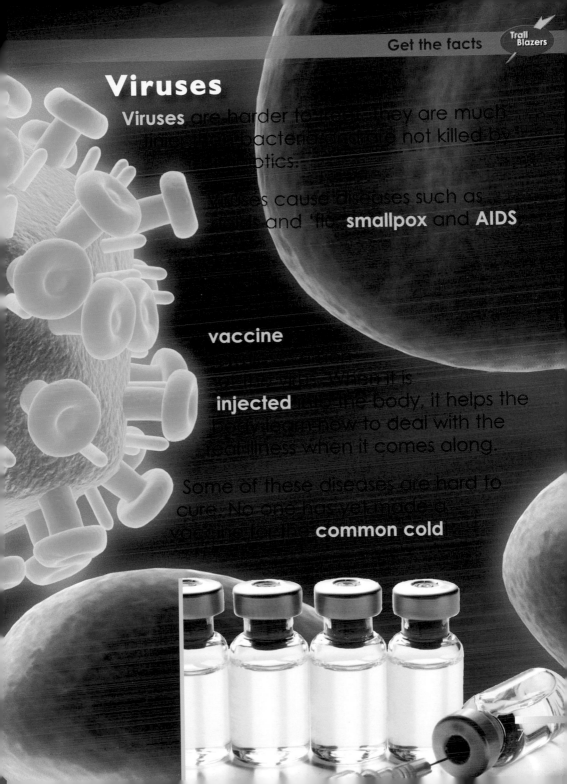

Animal plagues

Sometimes, huge numbers of animals such as **rats** or **flies** seem to appear from nowhere. We often call this a plague, though it's not really one at all.

Why does it happen?

Cane Toads

In **Australia**, **beetles** were **damaging** sugar cane crops.

So, in 1935, someone brought **cane toads** from **Hawaii** to eat them. This was a really bad idea!

The cane toads loved Australia. Now there are around a **hundred million** of them – and they are all hungry!

So what went wrong?

There are no animals in Australia that want to eat the toads. So there is nothing to control them.

Locusts

Locusts are grasshoppers. They fly in **great swarms**.

This is **bad news**. They will eat almost any plant, so crops can be ruined.

Why do they swarm?

Probably because the area they live in has become **overcrowded**.

Jellyfish

In November 2007, fish farms in **Ireland** were attacked by a huge swarm of stinging, purple-coloured jellyfish.

What was happening?

Scientists think the huge swarms of jellyfish may have something to do with **over-fishing** (boats catching too many fish in the Atlantic.)

9

The Black Death and the Great Plague

Plague fact file

The Black Death probably started in China around 1334. Soldiers and traders carried it to Europe. By 1348, it had reached England.

Between a third and a half of all people in Europe died.

The plague kept coming back for the next 300 years. The last outbreak in England was the Great Plague of 1665.

How did it start? No one really knows. Maybe it started because lots of animals moved to new areas because of a changing climate. This spread the disease.

So what is the plague anyway? Most scientists think all these deaths were caused by bubonic plague. Bubonic plague is caused by bacteria in the blood of rats and fleas.

If the bacteria get into a human's bloodstream, the person will get the plague.

And die? Not always. Many people who caught the plague got better. Now, the plague can be cured with antibiotics.

How did they try to cure the plague? All sorts of things: medical pokers, making people active doses ...

Did they work? No.

*A **plague doctor** from the time of the Great Plague.*

The costume was supposed to protect them.

Another cause –

Some scientists don't think it was bubonic plague. They say that the description of the disease doesn't match with what we know about it.

They say that there weren't any rats in some of the places hit by plague.

They think it might have been be caused by a virus, not by bacteria. If it was a virus, we may not be able to cure it.

Catching the 'flu

People think that **influenza** (the 'flu) is not a serious disease.

But in the years 1918-1919, it **killed** up to **100 million people** around the world.

Many young, healthy people died.

A 'flu hospital in *America, 1918.*

So what is 'flu?

'Flu is caused by a **virus**. Now we have a **vaccine** to stop us getting the 'flu.

So that's all right then?

Not quite.

The 'flu virus keeps **mutating** (changing). It can jump from **animals** to **humans**. Every year, it can be a little bit different.

This means that a vaccine won't always work.

What happens when you sneeze.
Yuk.

Modern plagues

Life is **much better** now than it was in the past.

People **live longer**.

A lot of deadly diseases can be cured. Diseases like **polio** and **smallpox** have disappeared altogether.

But **new diseases** are taking their place.

AIDS

AIDS first appeared in **Africa**, in the middle of the last century.

It is caused by a **virus**. AIDS stops the body fighting off other diseases. Over 25 million people around the world have died because they had AIDS.

Can it be cured?

No, but there are drugs that **help people** with AIDS live a normal life.

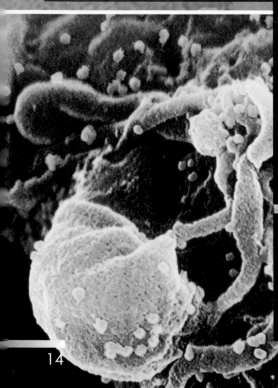

Ebola fever

This disease was first found in **Africa** in 1976. A virus attacks the main organs of the body.

Can it be cured?

No. Between 50 – 90% of people who catch it die.

Will it threaten the world?

Probably not.

Ebola fever is very **fast acting**. Usually outbreaks come and go quickly, staying in one small area.

'Flu from animals

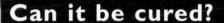

Bird 'flu kills birds such as **chickens**. Swine 'flu started in **pigs**.

These started as animal diseases. They have changed (**mutated**) so that people can be affected.

So what's the problem?

If a type of 'flu like this can pass from person to person, **millions of people** could be affected.

Where do plagues come from?

Many plagues start because animals move from the places where they are usually found.

Another reason is that there are more people in the world. This means there is more contact with wild animals.

Animal diseases can become human ones if the virus changes.

Two more problems

1 In the past, it could take weeks or months to travel to other countries. People might die before they could spread the disease.

Now you can go anywhere in the world in a few hours.

Diseases can spread quickly.

2 **Antibiotics** can cure diseases caused by **bacteria**.

Vaccines can stop people catching diseases caused by **viruses**.

But diseases keep **changing**. Scientists have to keep finding new ways to stop them.

Keeping diseases away is a battle we may never be able to win.

The Lost Village

Chapter 1:
Hedgestreet village,
October, 1347

That autumn, travellers passing through the village told stories of many people dying.

'They have great, black swellings on their bodies. Once this happens there is no hope. And it is a terrible death!'

Most of the villagers did not believe it. There was plenty of sickness, but nothing that matched this description. The villagers shrugged their shoulders and carried on with the hard work of bringing in the harvest.

Then one evening, Robin returned home from the fields to find his mother lying on her bed.

'What is it, mother?' he asked.

'It is just as the travellers told us! The black swellings! The pain is terrible!'

Robin rushed to find the village wise woman, but she too was struck down by the terrible sickness.

That night, Robin began to feel ill ...

A month later, there were only four people left in the village ...

Chapter 2:
Old Hedgestreet,
October, 2015

'This is Old Hedgestreet. Not much to see now, I'm afraid!'

Robin Banks and his class were on a history field trip. At first, all they could see was an empty field. Mrs Terry, their history teacher, told them to look closely.

'See all the humps and bumps? They show where the houses were. When the plague struck in October 1347, around two hundred people lived here. Almost all of them died of the plague.'

'Why didn't people come back to the village after the plague?'

'There were far fewer people in the country. Many villages were just abandoned like this.

'When the population grew again, they started a new village in a better place. That's the village we now call Hedgestreet, a mile away. That's where you live isn't it, Robin?'

Robin nodded. He looked at the humps and bumps and tried to imagine what it was like when the Black Death struck, all those years ago.

Chapter 3:
Hedgestreet village,
later that day

'Hi! I'm home!'

Robin's dad came into the hall, looking worried.

'Don't make a row, Robin. Your mum's asleep. I'm afraid she's not very well. It looks like a really bad case of 'flu. The doctor came round an hour ago. He says if it gets much worse she'll need to go to hospital.'

Later that day ...
I'm home!
Your mum's ill with the 'flu. She may have to go to hospital!

Robin's mum was beginning to find it hard to breathe. Dad rang for an ambulance.

'I'm sorry sir, I'm afraid the hospital is already full. There's not much we can do, I'm afraid.'

Robin and his dad sat with Mum all evening. No ambulance came.

The next morning, Robin woke up with a terrible headache. He was sweating with fever.

He staggered along to his parents' room.

'Mum, I'm ill!'

But there was no reply.

Chapter 4:
Hedgestreet,
October, 2350

'This is the site of Hedgestreet village. Look, you can still see parts of the walls, and even some of the old road that ran through the middle of it.

'When the 'flu virus struck in October 2015, around two thousand people lived here. Ninety percent of them died.'

'Why didn't people come back to the village after the 'flu?'

'There were far fewer people in the country. Many villages were just abandoned like this. When the population grew again they started a new village. That's the village we call New Hedgestreet. That's where you live isn't it, Robin?'

Robin nodded. He looked at the broken walls. Could it ever happen again?

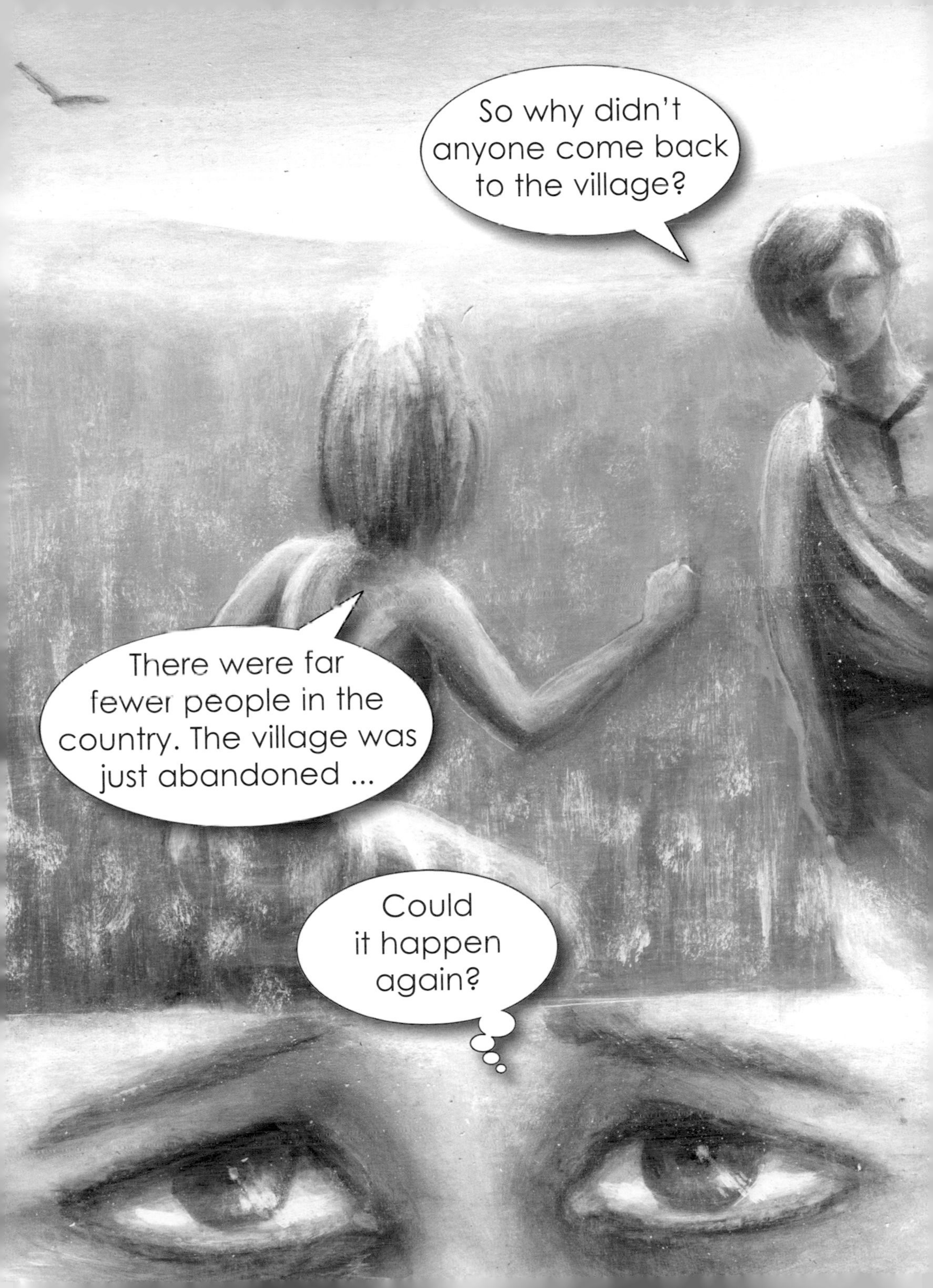

Plagues word che

abandoned

AIDS (Acquired Immune

Deficiency Syndrome)

antibiotics

bacteria

bacterium

Black Death

bloodstream

Bird 'flu

bubonic plague

disease

Ebola fever

'flu (influ

Great Pl

mutate

outbreak

polio

smallpox

swarm

Swine 'flu

TB (tuberculosis)

typhoid

vaccine

virus